E PLURIBUS UNUM

BY THE PEOPLE

STATE AND LOCAL GOVERNMENT

Bill McAuliffe

Creative Education ★ Creative Paperbacks

TABLE OF CONTENTS

★ ★ ★

"The true privilege of being mayor is that I have the opportunity to be everyone's neighbor," said former Boston mayor Thomas Menino.

STATE AND LOCAL GOVERNMENT

Menino was mayor for nearly 21 years, longer than anyone else in the city's history. During that time, he became famous for his close connection with residents—in a 2009 poll by the *Boston Globe*, nearly 60 percent of the respondents said they'd personally met him. He was also attentive to details such as potholes, abandoned cars, and how many kids had summer jobs. Menino was exceptionally successful, but his to-do list would be similar to that of most elected officials of state and local governments. However, in an era in which "big government" is often cast as a villain, the state and local versions, by being everywhere, are also like the neighbor you see every day. They are truly government of the people, by the people.

EARLY FORMS OF U.S. GOVERNMENT

1619

HOUSE OF BURGESSES

The colony of Virginia established a House of Burgesses in 1619. Members were elected by property owners in the colony. They passed their own laws, subject to approval by the king of England. It was the first legislature in the colonies.

MAYFLOWER COMPACT

English Puritans drew up the Mayflower Compact, named for their ship. It was the first written framework of government in what later became the U.S. It declared the group free of English law and remained in effect until 1691.

1620

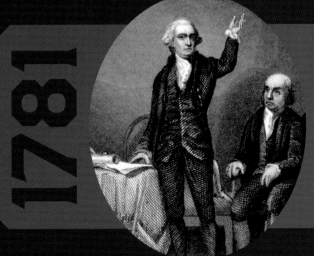

1781

ARTICLES OF CONFEDERATION

Following the Revolutionary War, the new country was governed by a document called the Articles of Confederation. Instead of giving too much power to a central, national government, the Articles set up a nation of loosely connected states.

CHAPTER 1

IT STARTED LOCALLY

STATE AND LOCAL GOVERNMENT

When the New World was first explored and settled, government seemed a distant thing. Lands were claimed by kingdoms across the oceans. But actual "control" was difficult, since the rulers were so far from their subjects. So a strong tradition of community self-government got started.

The colony of Virginia established a House of **Burgesses** in 1619. Members were elected by property owners in the colony. They passed their own laws, subject to approval by the king of England. It was the first legislature in the colonies.

The next year, English **Puritans** seeking religious freedom landed in Massachusetts. That was far north of the territory they'd aimed for, where laws were already in place. They needed to establish their own rules to avoid conflicts. So they drew up

★ **By 1732, there were 13 British colonies. Each had a charter recognizing the colony's status. But the king and his appointed governor kept full ruling authority.** ★

IT STARTED LOCALLY

the Mayflower Compact, named for their ship. It was the first written framework of government in what later became the United States. It declared the group free of English law and remained in effect until 1691.

Soon more people arrived, developing communities and businesses that demanded a much greater degree of organization. They needed roads, mail service, law enforcement, shipping and trade regulations, and policies for settling disputes and dealing with pirates. By 1732, there were 13 British colonies. Each had a charter recognizing the colony's status. But the king and his appointed governor kept full ruling authority. Most also had a legislature elected

by local landowners. This lawmaking body often controlled the governors' salaries. This often helped persuade governors to acknowledge the colonists' view of things.

Ultimately, the colonies declared their independence and fought a war to establish it. Then they had to design a new government. Following the Revolutionary War, the new country was governed by a document called the Articles of Confederation. Instead of giving too much power to a central, national government, the Articles set up a nation of loosely connected states. Within those states, most of the power was held by elected legislatures. Governors were regarded as a bad memory from colonial times, so they were weak or served

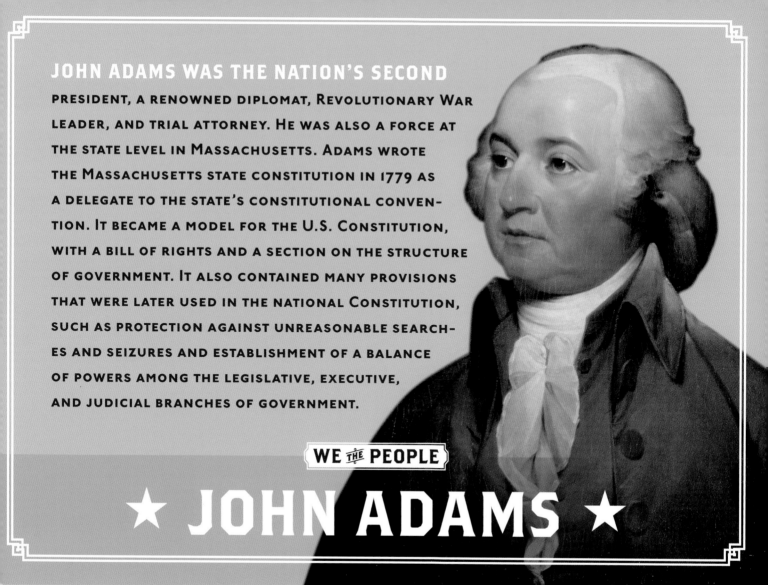

JOHN ADAMS WAS THE NATION'S SECOND PRESIDENT, A RENOWNED DIPLOMAT, REVOLUTIONARY WAR LEADER, AND TRIAL ATTORNEY. HE WAS ALSO A FORCE AT THE STATE LEVEL IN MASSACHUSETTS. ADAMS WROTE THE MASSACHUSETTS STATE CONSTITUTION IN 1779 AS A DELEGATE TO THE STATE'S CONSTITUTIONAL CONVENTION. IT BECAME A MODEL FOR THE U.S. CONSTITUTION, WITH A BILL OF RIGHTS AND A SECTION ON THE STRUCTURE OF GOVERNMENT. IT ALSO CONTAINED MANY PROVISIONS THAT WERE LATER USED IN THE NATIONAL CONSTITUTION, SUCH AS PROTECTION AGAINST UNREASONABLE SEARCHES AND SEIZURES AND ESTABLISHMENT OF A BALANCE OF POWERS AMONG THE LEGISLATIVE, EXECUTIVE, AND JUDICIAL BRANCHES OF GOVERNMENT.

WE THE PEOPLE

★ JOHN ADAMS ★

short terms. Some states didn't even have one. It wasn't long, though, before people began to sense that something wasn't right. States were acting almost as individual nations. There was no system to negotiate trade or other treaties as one nation. There was no national **monetary** system. There was no national defense.

So leaders scrapped the Articles of Confederation and drew up the U.S. Constitution. It went into effect in 1789. It curbed the powers of state legislatures. It established a federal government with a balance of power among an executive branch (the president), a legislative branch (Congress), and a judicial branch (the Supreme Court). It declared that the federal government had the power to collect taxes and pay debts, regulate international trade, set rules for achieving citizenship,

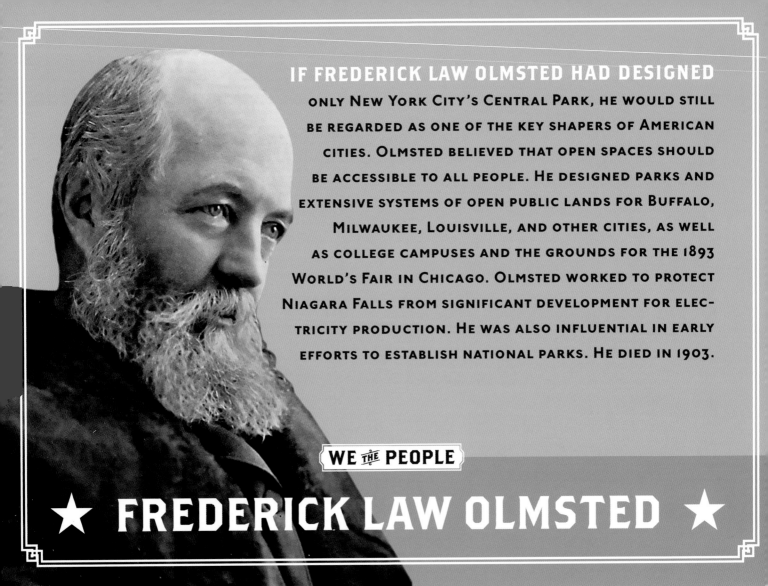

IF FREDERICK LAW OLMSTED HAD DESIGNED ONLY NEW YORK CITY'S CENTRAL PARK, HE WOULD STILL BE REGARDED AS ONE OF THE KEY SHAPERS OF AMERICAN CITIES. OLMSTED BELIEVED THAT OPEN SPACES SHOULD BE ACCESSIBLE TO ALL PEOPLE. HE DESIGNED PARKS AND EXTENSIVE SYSTEMS OF OPEN PUBLIC LANDS FOR BUFFALO, MILWAUKEE, LOUISVILLE, AND OTHER CITIES, AS WELL AS COLLEGE CAMPUSES AND THE GROUNDS FOR THE 1893 WORLD'S FAIR IN CHICAGO. OLMSTED WORKED TO PROTECT NIAGARA FALLS FROM SIGNIFICANT DEVELOPMENT FOR ELECTRICITY PRODUCTION. HE WAS ALSO INFLUENTIAL IN EARLY EFFORTS TO ESTABLISH NATIONAL PARKS. HE DIED IN 1903.

WE THE PEOPLE

★ FREDERICK LAW OLMSTED ★

coin money, establish post offices and post roads, declare war, form courts, establish **patents** and **copyrights**, and even to create standards for weights and measures.

But the 10th **Amendment** to the Constitution stated that any power not given to the national government or specifically denied to the states lies with the states. As it happens, that's a lot of powers. States share some powers with the federal government. Both levy taxes, borrow and spend money, protect civil rights, and establish courts. But states can do even more than that. They can regulate businesses and set professional standards, as in law or medicine. They can develop and maintain educational systems, and build universities. They can determine how old people must be before they can drive a car or drink alcohol. They can regulate nursing homes,

attack disease outbreaks, and enforce food safety standards. They can set standards for air and water pollution and enter into agreements with other states on issues such as climate change, air quality, and water use. They can provide parks and manage wildlife. They can run lotteries and license tattoo parlors. They

can operate prisons and, in extreme cases, execute people under the death penalty.

State agencies may preserve sites such as the Washington Crossing Historic Park.

States are free to organize their governments in different ways. New Hampshire's House of Representatives has 400 members. In Nevada, a state with more than twice as many people, its House has 42 members. Nebraska has

IT STARTED LOCALLY

the nation's only one-house, or "unicameral" legislature. It is also the only **nonpartisan** legislature. Its 49 senators, each representing a different **district**, make it the smallest legislature in the country.

State governments authorize more localized units of government. As states were formed, they divided themselves into counties, where courts, the sheriff, and other local officials were never more than a day's horseback ride from any resident's home. Today, there are more than 3,000 counties in the U.S. States also provide legal status to cities by granting them charters, which are almost like local constitutions. There are now about 19,000 such incorporated areas across the U.S. There are also about 16,000 township governments, operating in less-settled areas outside cities. Hawaii has only three counties and one **municipality**, the city of Honolulu. By contrast, Texas has 254 counties. Illinois has more than 2,700 municipalities.

States also authorize layer upon layer of agencies that often operate across city, county, and other borders, with specific missions. School districts are an example. As authors Bruce

> A legend of the American West, "Wild Bill" Hickok tamed two lawless Kansas towns as their sheriff or marshal.

The Works Progress Administration (WPA) was a federal work program that employed about 3 million Americans during the Great Depression.

FEDERAL GRANT MONEY   was provided for   STATE PROJECTS

AMERICANS BUILT

☞ public infrastructure such as buildings, bridges, and roads

☞ public works of art and parks

☞ AND MUCH MORE

THE WPA RAN LIBRARY PROJECTS IN 45 STATES.

Librarians were put to work repairing books as the Library Extension program worked to improve the accessibility of reading materials.

TRAVELING LIBRARIES

Traveling WPA librarians reached remote areas by any means necessary. Some librarians rode horses or mules into mountains, while others used boats to reach communities that were not connected by roads.

5,800
TRAVELING LIBRARIES

30 MILLION
BOOKS REPAIRED

200
NEW LIBRARIES BUILT

14,500
WORKERS EMPLOYED

FRANKLIN D. ROOSEVELT

IT STARTED LOCALLY

Katz and Jennifer Bradley describe it, state governments have created "a dizzying, often comical array of special-purpose entities: school districts, fire districts, library districts, sewer districts, mosquito districts, public benefit corporations, industrial development **authorities**, transportation authorities, ... control boards, and emergency financial managers." In 2012, there were approximately 90,000 local governmental bodies in the U.S. More than half were special-powers agencies. Many are run by elected officials. Many also have the power to levy taxes to fund their operations. They employ about 12 million people— perhaps 6 times as many as work for the federal government, excluding the Department of Defense.

In Kentucky, packhorse librarians provided reading materials to about 100,000 people in rural areas.

In the 1930s, as the Great Depression took hold across the U.S., local governments declined. People were unable to pay the taxes needed to support them. President Franklin D. Roosevelt's powerful federal programs of job creation and relief took their place.

But local government has become more important in recent decades. As taxpayers have demanded greater efficiency, state and local agencies have become more professional. They've hired experienced, well-educated, and often expensive administrators. Not long ago, the "dog catcher" was regarded as the lowliest, most solitary, and least significant official in local government. But he or she is now one of more than 12,000 "animal control officers" employed by U.S. municipalities.

GOVERNORS WHO WERE ELECTED PRESIDENT

ANDREW JOHNSON
17th President of the United States ★ 1865–69
Governor of Tennessee ★ 1853–57

THOMAS JEFFERSON
3rd President of the United States ★ 1801–09
Governor of Virginia ★ 1779–81

THEODORE ROOSEVELT
26th President of the United States ★ 1901–09
Governor of New York ★ 1899–1900

JIMMY CARTER
39th President of the United States ★ 1977–81
Governor of Georgia ★ 1971–75

JAMES MONROE
5th President of the United States ★ 1817–25 ★
Governor of Virginia ★ 1799–1802 , 1811

JOHN TYLER
10th President of the United States ★ 1841–45
Governor of Virginia ★ 1825–27

FRANKLIN D. ROOSEVELT
32nd President of the United States
★ 1933–45 ★
Governor of New York ★ 1929–32

WILLIAM McKINLEY
25th President of the United States ★ 1897–1901
Governor of Ohio ★ 1892–96

WOODROW WILSON
28th President of the United States ★ 1913–21
Governor of New Jersey ★ 1911–13

CALVIN COOLIDGE
30th President of the United States ★ 1923–29
Governor of Massachusetts ★ 1919–21

RONALD REAGAN
40th President of the United States ★ 1981–89
Governor of California ★ 1967–75

GROVER CLEVELAND
22nd & 24th President of the United States ★ 1885–89, 1893–97
Governor of New York ★ 1883–85

JAMES K. POLK
11th President of the United States ★ 1845–49
Governor of Tennessee ★ 1839–41

MARTIN VAN BUREN
8th President of the United States ★ 1837–41 ★
Governor of New York ★ 1829

GEORGE W. BUSH
43rd President of the United States ★ 1995–2000 ★ 2001–09
Governor of Texas ★ 1995–2000

RUTHERFORD B. HAYES
19th President of the United States ★ 1877–81
Governor of Ohio ★ 1868–72, 1876–77

BILL CLINTON
42nd President of the United States ★ 1993–2001
Governor of Arkansas ★ 1979–81, 1983–92

CHAPTER 2

STAR QUALITY

STATE AND LOCAL GOVERNMENT

At the head of each state's government is the governor. Governors have risen in stature since the early days of the nation, when many served only one- or two-year terms. Governors have become executives much like the president, managing the multibillion-dollar enterprises states have become. They appoint department heads and judges, develop state budgets, shape the legislature's agenda, and sometimes **veto** legislation. They also command their state's unit of the National Guard and authorize responses to disasters such as floods, forest fires, and blizzards. They can grant pardons to people who have been convicted of crimes. Politically, they are regarded as the head of their political party in their state, which can put them in a national spotlight. Seven former governors served in the cabinet of president George W. Bush, an ex-governor himself.

★ **To help combat the Great Depression, [Long] proposed plans to redistribute wealth. The program known as "Share Our Wealth" would have limited extremely high incomes while providing direct taxpayer support to poor families.** ★

STAR QUALITY

In 2014, salaries for governors ranged from $187,818 down to $70,000. Several governors return their salary to the state or have taken pay cuts. While this may show they are cutting expenses and protecting the taxpayer, it can also be a sign of personal wealth. Michigan governor Rick Snyder, elected to a second four-year term in 2014, returns all but $1 of his annual $159,300 salary, but he previously made his money in business.

Seventeen governors in U.S. history have stepped into the presidency, capitalizing on their experience as an executive at the state level. Four of the six presidents preceding Barack Obama had been governors before being elected president. But many governors have made an impression

on American history without ever becoming chief executive.

In 1928, Huey Long was elected governor of Louisiana. He served in the U.S. Senate from 1932 to 1935 but remained heavily involved in state government. He was so powerful, he became known as "The Kingfish." To help combat the Great Depression, he proposed plans to redistribute wealth. The program known as "Share Our Wealth" would have limited extremely high incomes while providing direct taxpayer support to poor families. Such ideas made him popular among working-class people. But they also created enemies. Long was assassinated by a political opponent's relative in 1935.

Show-business popularity has helped put

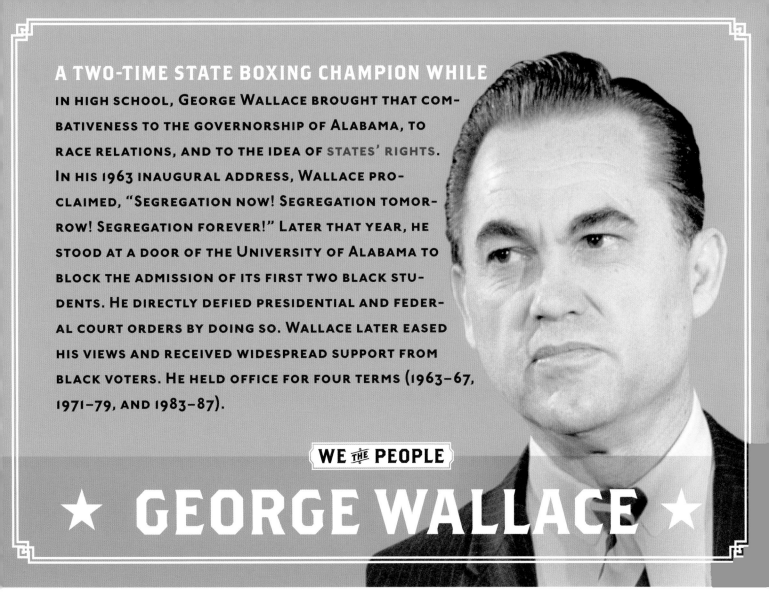

A TWO-TIME STATE BOXING CHAMPION WHILE IN HIGH SCHOOL, GEORGE WALLACE BROUGHT THAT COMBATIVENESS TO THE GOVERNORSHIP OF ALABAMA, TO RACE RELATIONS, AND TO THE IDEA OF STATES' RIGHTS. IN HIS 1963 INAUGURAL ADDRESS, WALLACE PROCLAIMED, "SEGREGATION NOW! SEGREGATION TOMORROW! SEGREGATION FOREVER!" LATER THAT YEAR, HE STOOD AT A DOOR OF THE UNIVERSITY OF ALABAMA TO BLOCK THE ADMISSION OF ITS FIRST TWO BLACK STUDENTS. HE DIRECTLY DEFIED PRESIDENTIAL AND FEDERAL COURT ORDERS BY DOING SO. WALLACE LATER EASED HIS VIEWS AND RECEIVED WIDESPREAD SUPPORT FROM BLACK VOTERS. HE HELD OFFICE FOR FOUR TERMS (1963–67, 1971–79, AND 1983–87).

WE THE PEOPLE

★ GEORGE WALLACE ★

people into elected office at the state and local level. John Davis Lodge starred in a number of successful Hollywood films in the 1930s. He was elected governor of Connecticut in 1951. Ronald Reagan had a long career in Hollywood films before becoming governor of California and then president. In 2003, California voters elected former bodybuilder and action film star Arnold Schwarzenegger to the first of two terms as governor.

Meanwhile, another action hero and accomplished film director, Clint Eastwood, served two years as mayor of Carmel-by-the-Sea, a small, artistic California town. He later was appointed to the California State Park and Recreation Commission. Singer Sonny Bono was mayor of Palm Springs, California, from 1988 to 1992 before being elected to the U.S. House of Representatives. The road between show business and politics has run the other

AFTER TWO TERMS IN THE U.S. HOUSE, ELLA GRASSO OF CONNECTICUT BECAME THE FIRST WOMAN ELECTED GOVERNOR IN HER OWN RIGHT IN 1974. GRASSO'S POPULARITY PEAKED DURING A HISTORIC SNOWSTORM IN 1978 WHEN SHE ABANDONED HER STUCK CAR AND WALKED THE FINAL MILE TO THE STATE ARMORY TO DECLARE ALL THE STATE'S ROADS CLOSED AND TO HELP WITH THE DISASTER RESPONSE. AS A STATE LEGISLATOR, SHE HAD LED A FIGHT TO ELIMINATE COUNTY GOVERNMENTS IN CONNECTICUT. MANY WANTED HER TO RUN FOR NATIONAL OFFICE. BUT AFTER BEING DIAGNOSED WITH CANCER, SHE RESIGNED AS GOVERNOR DECEMBER 31, 1980, AND DIED LESS THAN TWO MONTHS LATER.

WE THE PEOPLE

★ ELLA GRASSO ★

way, too. Jerry Springer was briefly the mayor of Cincinnati, Ohio, before becoming host of a wildly popular television talk show in the 1990s.

The first female governor was Nellie Tayloe Ross of Wyoming. She was elected in 1924 to succeed her husband, who had died in office. Two weeks after Ross was sworn in, Miriam A. Ferguson became governor of Texas in January 1925. She'd been elected

after her husband was **impeached**. The first woman elected governor without following in a husband's footsteps was Connecticut's Ella Grasso (1975–80).

P.B.S. Pinchback, former lieutenant governor of Louisiana, became the nation's first black governor for 36 days in 1872 and 1873. (During that time, the elected governor underwent an impeachment trial.) It would be more than 100 years before voters elected a

Former mayor and governor Grover Cleveland lost the presidential race in 1888.

black governor. That was Douglas Wilder (1990–94) in Virginia.

There has never been a **sitting** American mayor who has become president. (Grover Cleveland is the only former mayor ever elected president, but that followed his days as governor of Ohio.) Some say that's because mayors have to make many decisions that can be used against them in a run for higher office. But mayor Charlie Hales of Portland, Oregon, thinks mayors would make good presidents because they tend to be nonpartisan problem solvers. "There's no such thing as a Republican pothole or a Democratic sewer problem," Hales said.

FIORELLO LA GUARDIA

★ **Many mayors have achieved national attention while overseeing complicated city governments and political landscapes.** ★

═══ STAR QUALITY ═══

Many mayors have achieved national attention while overseeing complicated city governments and political landscapes. And, like governors, they have frequently put the stamp of their own personality on their community, for better or worse. Former New York City mayor Fiorello La Guardia was ranked the best big-city mayor in history by *Time* magazine in 2005. Historian Melvin Holli had already suggested it in his 1999 book, *The American Mayor: The Best & the Worst Big-City Leaders*. La Guardia had served several terms in the U.S. House of Representatives

by the time he was elected mayor in 1934. The feisty, 5-foot-2 man, nicknamed "The Little Flower," was the first Italian American mayor in the city's history. He constantly battled the influence of Italian- and Irish-led organized crime. Early in his term, he had thousands of **mob**-owned slot machines seized and personally destroyed them with a sledgehammer as they were being hauled to sea on a barge. He also steadily converted the way city employees were hired, moving away from a system based on political favoritism to one based on merit. During a newspaper strike, he read the

> In 1934, Mayor La Guardia literally brought down the hammer on mob-related businesses such as the slot machines.

TOP AND BOTTOM FIVE GOVERNOR SALARIES IN 2014

Pennsylvania	$187,818
Tennessee	$181,000
New York	$179,000
Illinois	$177,412
New Jersey	$175,000
Oregon	$98,600
Arizona	$95,000
Colorado	$90,000
Arkansas	$86,890
Maine	$70,000

WILLIAM HALE THOMPSON

comics pages to residents over the radio.

By contrast, Holli cites Chicago's mayor William Hale "Big Bill" Thompson as the worst mayor in U.S. history. Three-time Mayor Thompson (1915–23 and 1927–31) received campaign funds from known gangsters, expressed sympathy for Germany during World War I, and called opponents names during campaigns. The *Chicago Tribune* wrote that Thompson had "given the city an international reputation for moronic buffoonery, barbaric crime, triumphant hoodlumism, unchecked **graft**, and a dejected citizenship."

Sometimes the unelected officials are the ones who become the most powerful in local governments. In the process, they reshape their communities. The best example of this is probably New York's Robert Moses. From 1924 to 1968, Moses held numerous appointed positions with New York City and New York State authorities and commissions. He managed to finance and oversee the construction of bridges, roads, parks, and housing projects that transformed the city. Many of the projects were authorized without any voter input, though. This has led to criticism that Moses damaged neighborhoods and was undemocratic.

> Not counting the three governors who refused or refunded their salaries, the table opposite shows the highest and lowest figures for 2014.

ZONING

★ SCHOOLS ★

PUBLIC LIBRARIES

FIRE DEPARTMENT

MARRIAGE CERTIFICATES

COURTS

PARKS AND RECREATION

PROPERTY TAXES

ROADS AND BRIDGES

★ POLICE DEPARTMENT ★

CHAPTER 3

WHO'S ON THE JOB?

STATE AND LOCAL GOVERNMENT

When the weather forecast calls for snow overnight, school superintendents suddenly become the most powerful people in town. Well before dawn, they can be found on the phone with the weather service, the school bus company, and the local public works department. They try to determine how hard it might be to get kids to school later that morning. If they decide to call off school, parents will have to stay home from work or call babysitters. Kids will miss tests, games, and practices. The lives of many families in town will be disrupted.

Most decisions by local governments are unlike closing schools during a storm. They usually require months of meetings, reviews, debates, and votes before being carried out. But they all demonstrate that local governments can have an impact at a personal and neighborhood level. Local governments and

★ **Counties can have very different characteristics from one another. Loving County, in west Texas, had 82 residents in 2010. California's Los Angeles County had 9.8 million!** ★

WHO'S ON THE JOB?

their boards and agencies can change the equipment at the corner playground, restore the bends in the creek that runs through the city, and determine what's available on the Internet at the public library. They can make sure one divorced parent makes child support payments to the other. More broadly, they can decide whether an area should have apartments or single-family homes. They can choose whether that weedy stretch where freight trains used to run should be used for a bike trail or a commuter railroad.

The governments most people are familiar with are based on geography: states, counties, and cities. But there are many others that aren't obvious from looking at a map. School districts often draw students from several cities, towns, and **unincorporated** areas. Watershed districts are places defined by where rainwater goes after it falls. The Woodsy Lake Watershed District, for example, would be where rainwater flows into creeks and rivers that feed into Woodsy Lake. Residents there would pay taxes to the district to manage such things as the flow and pollution levels of the water. There might be similar arrangements for sewer operations, fire protection, parks, and drinking water.

When people are asked where they live, they often list their city and state but not their county. Counties are less well known. In some states, they are not even

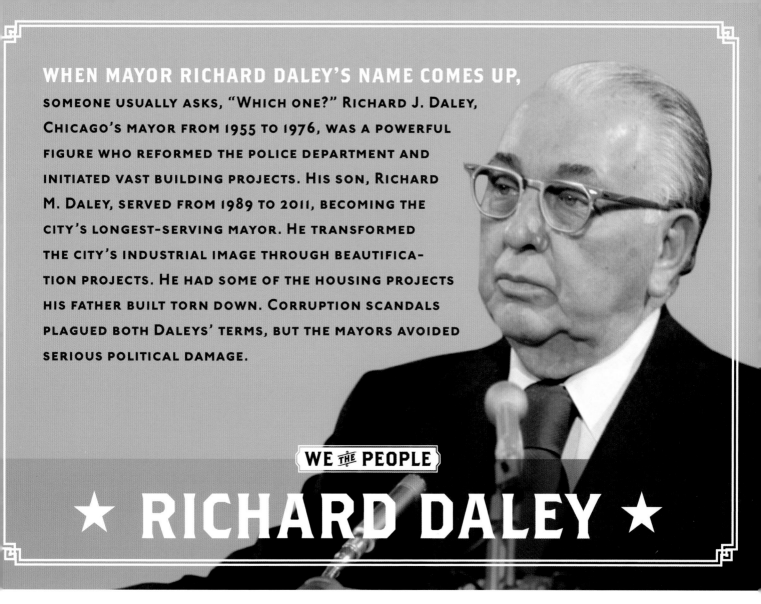

★ RICHARD DALEY ★

WHEN MAYOR RICHARD DALEY'S NAME COMES UP, SOMEONE USUALLY ASKS, "WHICH ONE?" RICHARD J. DALEY, CHICAGO'S MAYOR FROM 1955 TO 1976, WAS A POWERFUL FIGURE WHO REFORMED THE POLICE DEPARTMENT AND INITIATED VAST BUILDING PROJECTS. HIS SON, RICHARD M. DALEY, SERVED FROM 1989 TO 2011, BECOMING THE CITY'S LONGEST-SERVING MAYOR. HE TRANSFORMED THE CITY'S INDUSTRIAL IMAGE THROUGH BEAUTIFICATION PROJECTS. HE HAD SOME OF THE HOUSING PROJECTS HIS FATHER BUILT TORN DOWN. CORRUPTION SCANDALS PLAGUED BOTH DALEYS' TERMS, BUT THE MAYORS AVOIDED SERIOUS POLITICAL DAMAGE.

called counties. In Louisiana, they are called "parishes." In Alaska, they're "boroughs." Counties can have very different characteristics from one another. Loving County, in west Texas, had 82 residents in 2010. California's Los Angeles County had 9.8 million! But counties are where government starts getting really close to people.

Counties are usually run by a board of three to five elected officials. Most have an elected sheriff who provides law enforcement outside the cities. The sheriff operates the county jail. Most people who get arrested for a crime have their first court hearing before a county judge. They are formally accused of the crime by a county attorney, also known as a county prosecutor. Meanwhile, the county clerk registers **deeds** to homes. The county assessor determines how much properties are worth

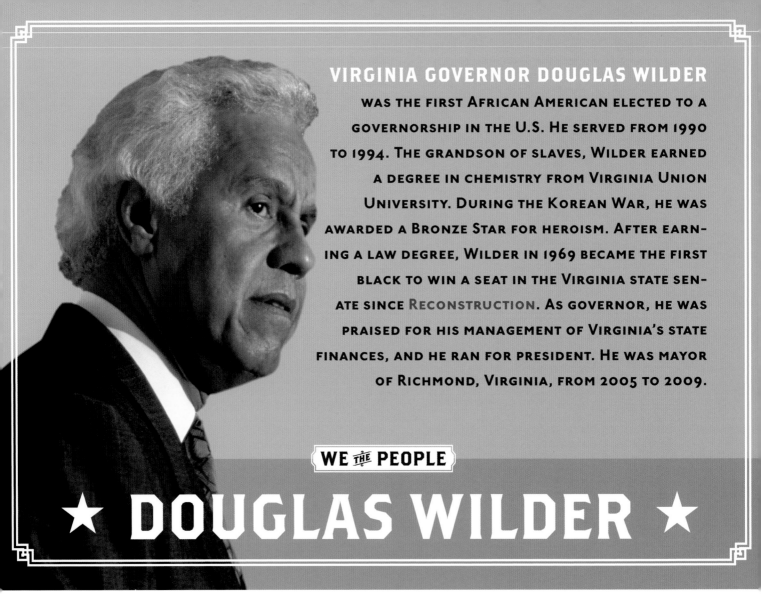

VIRGINIA GOVERNOR DOUGLAS WILDER WAS THE FIRST AFRICAN AMERICAN ELECTED TO A GOVERNORSHIP IN THE U.S. HE SERVED FROM 1990 TO 1994. THE GRANDSON OF SLAVES, WILDER EARNED A DEGREE IN CHEMISTRY FROM VIRGINIA UNION UNIVERSITY. DURING THE KOREAN WAR, HE WAS AWARDED A BRONZE STAR FOR HEROISM. AFTER EARNING A LAW DEGREE, WILDER IN 1969 BECAME THE FIRST BLACK TO WIN A SEAT IN THE VIRGINIA STATE SENATE SINCE RECONSTRUCTION. AS GOVERNOR, HE WAS PRAISED FOR HIS MANAGEMENT OF VIRGINIA'S STATE FINANCES, AND HE RAN FOR PRESIDENT. HE WAS MAYOR OF RICHMOND, VIRGINIA, FROM 2005 TO 2009.

WE THE PEOPLE

★ DOUGLAS WILDER ★

so that homeowners know how much they have to pay in taxes. Some counties, mostly those with large cities, employ a coroner. This person determines the causes of people's deaths in murders, accidents, or in mysterious situations. Counties also build and maintain roads and bridges. They may coordinate waste disposal and recycling, too. Many rural counties even have a "weed commissioner," whose job it is to locate and destroy harmful weeds, including plants such as marijuana.

Counties may be best known as providers of social services, from child protection, mental health, and chemical dependency programs to cash-support programs that help low-income people buy food and pay rent. Many of these programs are created by federal and state governments but administered by counties.

In 18 states, counties are further subdivided into townships. These square areas often measure 6 miles (9.7 km) on each side. In places such as Iowa, there are often 16 townships per county. In the past, each township often provided a single, one-room school. Today, many maintain a township hall, where a township board of three to five elected officials meets to discuss public business. The hall often serves as a polling place on election day.

Throughout New England and in Wisconsin, townships are known as towns. Community members gather at town meetings to vote on local laws and tax rates. They decide what to

Once the norm in education, nearly 200 one-room schoolhouses still operate today.

★ Numerous other bodies serve as extensions of local government and are often described as quasi-governmental. ★

spend money on. This type of government, though rare today, is rooted in American history and is known as direct democracy.

Villages are another form of municipality. The term is defined differently from state to state. Skokie, Illinois, is regarded as the world's largest village. With more than 65,000 residents, Skokie is bigger than many American towns and cities.

Other arms of local government are often little-known but have some elected officials and the ability to tax. They focus on things such as transportation, gas and

The Port Authority of New York & New Jersey maintains local infrastructure such as the George Washington Bridge.

electric service, airports, and even cemeteries. And they are plentiful. The number of special districts in the U.S. more than tripled from 1952 to 2012. There are now an average of more than 765 special districts in each state and more than 12 in every county, according to the Census Bureau.

Numerous other bodies serve as extensions of local government and are often described as quasi-governmental. This means they appear to be like the government. They often have some elected officials among their directors. Many have the word "authority" in their

GOVERNMENT EMPLOYEES, MARCH 2013

Federal, state, and local governments employed

21.8 million

☞ Most government workers are employed by one of the nearly 90,000 local governments in the U.S.

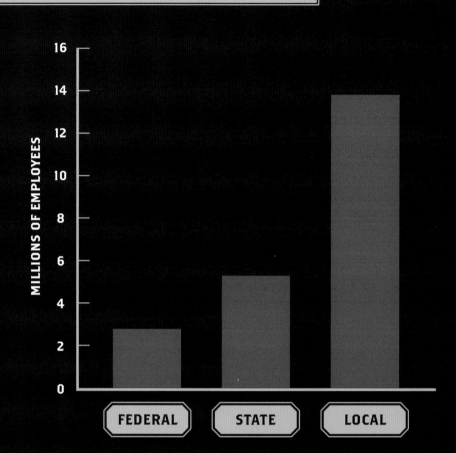

MILLIONS OF EMPLOYEES

FEDERAL STATE LOCAL

GOVERNMENT EDUCATION EMPLOYEES

FEDERAL	0.1 MILLION
STATE	2.7 MILLION
LOCAL	8.1 MILLION
TOTAL	10.9 MILLION

☞ Government education employees accounted for nearly half the total government workforce in 2013.

BOSTON LATIN SCHOOL

name. Port authorities are some of the most common. They often operate local transportation or shipping facilities, providing a stage to support private businesses and collecting fees. But they are also frequently involved in industrial development that has little to do with "ports." They may buy and clear land to make way for new factories or office parks.

That school superintendent who was thinking about calling a snow day directs 1 of 14,000 public school districts providing elementary and high school education in the U.S. The first school district was formed in 1647, when Massachusetts ordered towns to provide education. Ever since, school districts have been where local values and identities are argued about and formed, perhaps more so than at any other level of government. School boards and parents regularly debate what should be taught in their schools. They sometimes take issue with political and moral content of art and science materials. Politicians' cries for increasing "local control" often spring from school issues. Some say that as federal and state governments exercise more authority over public enterprises, school districts are becoming some of the last places where a community can have real control of a public agency.

The first public school, Boston Latin School (pictured c. 1748–1810) predated the first school district by 12 years.

NEW HAVEN, CONNECTICUT, CITY HALL AND COURTHOUSE IN 1861

CHAPTER 4

NEW DESIGNS FOR LOCAL GOVERNMENTS

STATE AND LOCAL GOVERNMENT

In many American communities, one of the most distinctive buildings is the county courthouse. Of course, that handsome stone structure is often the *old* courthouse. The new courthouse is often a broad, low building, surrounded by parking lots. Its distinguishing feature might be its walls of glass. In large cities, courthouses are often tall towers. And if they look like office buildings, that's fitting. Governments are often some of the biggest employers in town.

County government has slowly but dramatically gained prominence. The increase in car ownership after World War I led people to explore life outside the cities. Counties then had to improve roads, parks, and other government services. In the 1950s, older major cities peaked in population, and suburban populations exploded. Inexpensive land, lower taxes, cleaner air, and more space for recreation and home-building lured people out of

★ **In 2014, a group of more than 2,000 staged a protest at the Mall of America.... Authorities argued that the enclosed mall was private property and not a public square.** ★

NEW DESIGNS FOR LOCAL GOVERNMENTS

cities at that time. Industries moved out as well, for many of the same reasons. Shopping centers followed them. Meanwhile, the federal government poured money into the interstate highway system, making it easier to transport people and goods. The 2010 census found that 51 percent of the nation's people lived in suburbs, more than double the percentage in 1950. That has added a tremendous workload to local governments in those areas.

One intriguing development related to those trends has been the rise of the so-called

> Every year, more than 40 million people visit the Mall of America, which has been open since 1992.

"edge city," a term invented by author Joel Garreau. Edge cities are places more or less created by new highways, where large office parks, shopping malls, and industrial parks have covered former farmland. These developments are often technically governed by the county. But in reality, a more direct and active authority is exerted by local businesses in a kind of "shadow government," Garreau notes. This provides security, assesses fees for parking and maintenance, and establishes land-use regulations usually set by elected government officials. In 2014, a group of more than

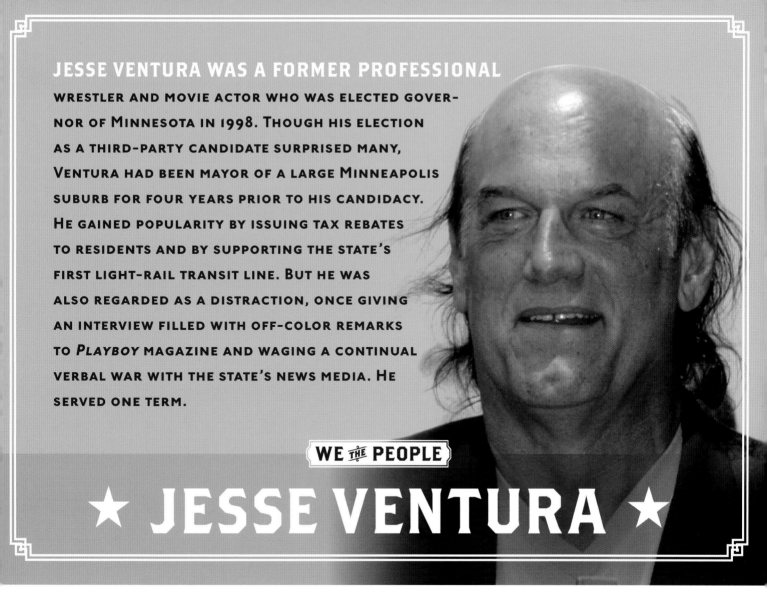

★ JESSE VENTURA ★

JESSE VENTURA WAS A FORMER PROFESSIONAL WRESTLER AND MOVIE ACTOR WHO WAS ELECTED GOVERNOR OF MINNESOTA IN 1998. THOUGH HIS ELECTION AS A THIRD-PARTY CANDIDATE SURPRISED MANY, VENTURA HAD BEEN MAYOR OF A LARGE MINNEAPOLIS SUBURB FOR FOUR YEARS PRIOR TO HIS CANDIDACY. HE GAINED POPULARITY BY ISSUING TAX REBATES TO RESIDENTS AND BY SUPPORTING THE STATE'S FIRST LIGHT-RAIL TRANSIT LINE. BUT HE WAS ALSO REGARDED AS A DISTRACTION, ONCE GIVING AN INTERVIEW FILLED WITH OFF-COLOR REMARKS TO *PLAYBOY* MAGAZINE AND WAGING A CONTINUAL VERBAL WAR WITH THE STATE'S NEWS MEDIA. HE SERVED ONE TERM.

2,000 staged a protest at the Mall of America in Bloomington, Minnesota. The group's organizers thought they were exercising their rights to free speech and assembly. But they were arrested. Authorities argued that the enclosed mall was private property and not a public square.

In recent decades, counties have taken on more and more tasks. In many states, they now handle traditionally urban functions such as transportation, water distribution, sewer operations, and land-use planning.

Counties have long been seen as a layer of government that didn't really fit anywhere. Journalist Ellen Perlman notes that, as a result, they've supported a variety of officials and agencies that have often produced needless jurisdictional conflicts. They've created duplication in purchasing and costs, and they've resisted the introduction of modern

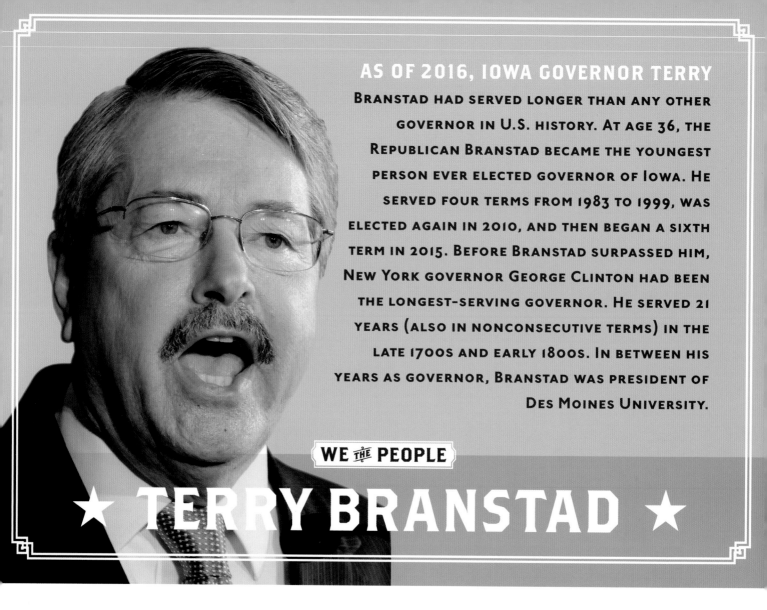

WE THE PEOPLE

★ TERRY BRANSTAD ★

personnel systems, Perlman adds. But with broader boundaries than cities, counties are increasingly better able to tackle problems that are difficult for cities to address. County executives may also bring a higher level of expertise and efficiency to the job than in the past. As urban populations continue to expand, they can involve multiple counties in their area of influence. Sometimes they even extend across jurisdictional lines, where

taxes, housing regulations, and services differ wildly. Missouri's St. Louis metro area, for example, includes the city, 15 counties, 272 smaller cities, 107 townships, 136 school districts, and 411 special districts in 2 states. This can present challenges for residents as well as local governments themselves.

In some places, cities and counties have combined into one governmental entity. San Francisco, Indianapolis, Philadelphia,

and Denver are some of the best known. In the Minneapolis–St. Paul metro area, the Minnesota legislature 50 years ago authorized the formation of the Metropolitan Council. It is a planning and management agency for a seven-county metro area. The council, run by 16 people appointed by the governor, manages regional wastewater collection and treatment, mass transit, and low-income housing distribution.

The city of San Francisco was the county seat until 1856, when a city-county government began.

According to Perlman, the trend toward city-county consolidation is likely to continue. It fits with people's demands for more services and with their unwillingness to pay more taxes. Consolidation has already

> ★ **Some of the challenges state governments will be facing in the near future are already obvious.... They'll also be striving to address increasing immigration rates, higher costs for education, and environmental issues surrounding gas and oil mining.** ★

NEW DESIGNS FOR LOCAL GOVERNMENTS

taken place to a great extent among school districts. In 1952, the nation had almost 70,000 public school districts. In 2012, there were 14,000, and they were generally much bigger than the old ones. Taxpayers have welcomed the savings in building costs and salaries. And parents have appreciated the increase in educational and extracurricular opportunities for their kids. But many have lamented the loss of smaller, local high schools and the strong local identities they had.

Some of the challenges state governments will be facing in the near future

> About $480 of the $12,400 spent annually on each public school student goes to transportation costs.

are already obvious. Instituting universal healthcare is at the top of the list. They'll also be striving to address increasing immigration rates, higher costs for education, and environmental issues surrounding gas and oil mining. States and cities will also have to confront the tensions between law enforcement and minorities, and the demand for alternative forms of transportation. They'll have to figure out how to regulate new types of businesses, such as app-based taxi services. Meanwhile, cities and counties have already become "central actors" in developing ways to deal with

STATE GOVERNMENT CHALLENGES

UNIVERSAL HEALTHCARE

Providing healthcare to citizens and implementing and enforcing the federal Affordable Care Act.

GAS AND OIL MINING

Determining how to regulate gas and oil mining while monitoring the effects on the environment.

EDUCATION

Providing up-to-date facilities, technology, and materials as well as sufficient educators and classroom aides.

IMMIGRATION

Effecting policies and programs that serve both native- and foreign-born members of communities.

BUSINESS REGULATIONS

Enforcing restrictions, various licenses, and other regulations.

CLIMATE CHANGE

Working to reduce pollution and emissions and promoting the research and use of renewable resources.

NEW DESIGNS FOR LOCAL GOVERNMENTS

the effects of climate change, according to Brian Gerber, an associate professor of pubic affairs at the University of Colorado. Many have begun assessing how increased rainfall and temperature differences might test their sewer systems, health programs, and emergency responses.

At the same time, the old push and pull between the federal and state and local governments is not about to cease. Local governments are likely to continue to serve as testing grounds for possible federal regulations. But they're also likely to defy them. Before president Barack Obama signed the Affordable Care Act, three states had their own versions. They were models for the national plan. But in 2012, Utah turned down $76 million in federal money rather than

> As natural disasters more frequently affect vulnerable areas, state and local governments become first responders.

agree to implement the federal No Child Left Behind program in its schools.

Those issues, along with the increasing size and scope of local government, suggest that it's unlikely that the mayor of any major U.S. city will ever again be able to personally meet half its residents. But as long as people are willing to participate, they can energize local democracy.

"If government by the people is to be more than just rhetoric [words], citizens must understand state and local politics and be willing to form political alliances ... and be willing to serve as citizen leaders and citizen politicians," write the authors of *State and Local Politics: Government by the People*. "Every person can make a difference."

amendment a change, clarification, or addition to the U.S. Constitution, proposed by Congress and approved by three-fourths of the states

authorities governmental agencies that administer a specific task, such as a "transit authority"

Burgesses elected or appointed officials of a municipality in colonial Virginia or Maryland, or in the British Parliament

coin to make money out of metal

copyrights forms of government protection for original writings, music, designs, maps, etc., limiting use or sale by anyone other than the author or the author's agent for a set period

deeds documents that prove ownership of a piece of property

district a geographical or political division made for a specific purpose

graft illegal practices, especially bribery, used to secure gains in politics or business

impeached charged with crimes committed while in office, which can lead to an elected official's removal

mob another word for organized crime

monetary having to do with money

municipality a local unit of government authorized by a state and smaller than a county, such as a city, township, village, borough, etc.

nonpartisan not attached to or identified with a political party

patents exclusive rights given to an inventor to make or sell an invention

Puritans members of the Anglican Church who believed the church was not living up to its values and wanted to separate from it

Reconstruction the period after the Civil War; the term refers to an overhaul of the economic, political, and social structures of the former Confederate States of America

sitting holding office

states' rights powers granted to the states by the Constitution and an idea used throughout history to justify opposition to federal measures, particularly those involving slavery and civil rights

unincorporated not governed by its own charter or municipal corporation but by a larger entity, such as a township or county

veto a cancellation by an executive of a measure approved by others

SELECTED BIBLIOGRAPHY

Christensen, Terry, and Tom Hogen-Esch. *Local Politics: A Practical Guide to Governing at the Grassroots.* 2nd ed. Armonk, N.Y.: M. E. Sharpe, 2006.

Fonder, Melanie, and Mary Shaffrey. *The Complete Idiot's Guide to American Government.* 2nd ed. New York: Penguin, 2005.

Garreau, Joel. *Edge City: Life on the New Frontier.* New York: Doubleday, 1991.

Katz, Bruce, and Jennifer Bradley. *The Metropolitan Revolution: How Cities and Metros are Fixing our Broken Politics and Fragile Economy.* Washington, D.C.: Brookings Institution, 2013.

Magleby, David B., David M. O'Brien, Paul C. Light, J. W. Peltason, and Thomas E. Cronin. *State and Local Politics: Government by the People.* 13th ed. Upper Saddle River, N.J.: Pearson, 2008.

Monkkonen, Eric H. *America Becomes Urban: The Development of U.S. Cities and Towns 1780–1980.* Berkeley: University of California Press, 1988.

WEBSITES

Ducksters: State and Local Governments
www.ducksters.com/history/us_state_and_local_governments.php
Learn more about different types of governments, and take a quiz.

Great Government for Kids
www.cccoe.net/govern/
Go on an online scavenger hunt and do other activities to investigate how local governments work.

Note: Every effort has been made to ensure that the websites listed above are suitable for children, that they have educational value, and that they contain no inappropriate material. However, because of the nature of the Internet, it is impossible to guarantee that these sites will remain active indefinitely or that their contents will not be altered.

Published by **Creative Education** and **Creative Paperbacks** P.O. Box 227, Mankato, Minnesota 56002 Creative Education and Creative Paperbacks are imprints of **The Creative Company** www.thecreativecompany.us

Design and production by **Christine Vanderbeek** Art direction by **Rita Marshall** Printed in China

Photographs by Corbis (Bettmann, CORBIS, K.J. Historical, Pete Saloutos, Tim Wright), Creative Commons Wikimedia (William Beechey/National Portrait Gallery, Boston Public Latin School, Jean Leon Gerome Ferris/Library of Congress, Harris & Ewing/ Library of Congress, Historical American Buildings Survey/ Library of Congress, IowaPolitics. com, Emanuel Leutze/Metropolitan Museum of Art, James Notman, Office of History and Preservation/ U.S. House of Representatives, John R. Penniman, South Carolina State Library/U.S. Federal Government, Marion S. Trikosko/Library of Congress, John Trumbull/ The White House Historical Association, U.S. National Archives and Records Administration), Dreamstime (Yanmingzhang), Getty Images (Peter J. Eckel, National Geographic), iStockphoto (ChrisSteer), Shutterstock (carrie-nelson, Robert Crum, Everett Historical, javarman, Ikeskinen)

Library of Congress Cataloging-in-Publication Data McAuliffe, Bill. State and Local Government / Bill McAuliffe. p. cm. — (By the people) Includes bibliographical references and index. *Summary*: A historical survey of state and local governments, including the role and responsibilities each has in its community and influential mayors, governors, and others.

ISBN 978-1-60818-674-7 *(hardcover)* **ISBN** 978-1-62832-270-5 *(pbk)* **ISBN** 978-1-56660-710-0 *(eBook)*

1. State governments—United States—Juvenile literature. 2. Local government—United States—Juvenile literature.

JK2408.M43 2016 320.473—dc23   2015039273

CCSS: RI.5.1, 2, 3, 8; RI. 6.1, 2, 4, 7; RH.6-8.3, 4, 5, 6, 7, 8

First Edition HC 9 8 7 6 5 4 3 2 1 **First Edition PBK** 9 8 7 6 5 4 3 2 1

Pictured on cover: John Adams